CATS
SET II

Devon Rex Cats

Stuart A. Kallen
ABDO & Daughters

visit us at
www.abdopublishing.com

Published by Abdo & Daughters, 8000 West 78th Street, Edina, Minnesota 55439
Copyright © 1998 by Abdo Consulting Group, Inc. International copyrights reserved in
all countries. No part of this book may be reproduced in any form without written permission
from the publisher.

Printed in the United States of America, North Mankato, Minnesota.
011998 052012
Photo credits: Peter Arnold, Inc., Animals Animals, TICA

Edited by Lori Kinstad Pupeza

Library of Congress Cataloging-in-Publication Data

Kallen, Stuart A., 1955-
    Devon rex cats / Stuart A. Kallen
    p. cm. -- (Cats. Set II)
    Includes index.
    Summary: Presents Information about the breed of cat that was first discovered
in Devon, England, in 1960 and which is distinguished by a pizie-like face.
    ISBN 1-56239-580-7
    1. Rex cat--Juvenile literature. [1. Rex cat. 2. Cats.] I. Title. II. Series: Kallen,
Stuart A., 1955- Cats. Set II.
    SF449.R4K34 1998
    686.8'2--dc20
                                 95-48190
                                   CIP
                                   AC

Contents

Lions, Tigers, and Cats

Few animals are as beautiful and graceful as cats. All kinds of cats are related. From the wild lions of Africa to common house cats, all belong to the family *Felidae*. Wild cats are found almost everywhere. They include cheetahs, jaguars, lynx, ocelots, and **domestic** cats.

Cats were first domesticated around 5,000 years ago in the Middle East. Although tamed by humans, house cats still think and act like their bigger cousins.

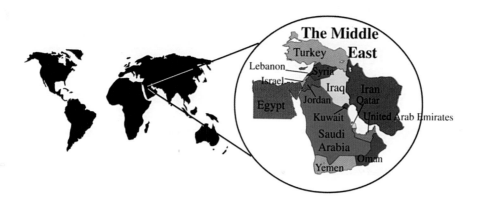

The Middle East

4

Wild cats are related to domestic cats.

The Devon Rex

The Devon rex is a cat who looks like no other. They are said to look like pixies with huge ears and eyes on small heads. Devons have short, wavy coats. People love Devons because they look like kittens, even when they are full grown!

Devons were first discovered by a woman in Devon, England in 1960. The woman noticed a curly haired cat near her home. It bred with her cat and one of the kittens had a similar, curly coat. Excited by the discovery, the woman continued to breed the cat. Soon, **Cat Fanciers** realized they had a new **breed** of cat. Devons were first **registered** as a breed in 1979.

The Devon rex is a unique looking cat.

Qualities

People who like the unusual will prize the Devon rex. Their pixie-like faces match their charm. Devons like to "talk" and make playful pets. Devons are excellent climbers. They are not fragile, but like a light touch when petted. Devons love people but do not get along well with other pets.

Most cats wave their tails from side to side when they are mad. But the Devon does this when it is happy. And they have devoted personalities like dogs. They also play "fetch." These traits, plus their curly coats, have led some people to call Devons "poodle cats."

Devon rex: the poodle cat.

Coat and Color

The wavy coat of a Devon rex is fuzzy and feels like suede or corduroy. The underparts of the cat may be covered with down-like fur. Kittens do not develop full coats until they are 18 months of age. Devons may shed quite a bit of fur. This may leave bald spots on the cat. This is normal and is not a cause for worry. Devons have crinkled, brittle whiskers that may break off.

The Devon rex come in many colors. A white cat with gold eyes is the most common type of Devon. Other colors and markings include black, blue, red, cream, smoke, classic tabby, mackerel tabby, silver, brown, patched tabby, and tortoiseshell.

The coat of a Devon rex is short and fuzzy.

Size

The Devon rex is a medium size cat, weighing between 5 and 10 pounds (2 to 4.5 kg). Devons have very slender necks and bodies. They have broad chests and hard, muscular bodies.

Devons have long, thin legs and small, round paws. Their eyes are large, oval, and set well apart. Their eyes slope toward the edges of their large, broad ears. Devons have short, wedge-shaped faces with large cheeks. Their ears are quite big for the size of their faces.

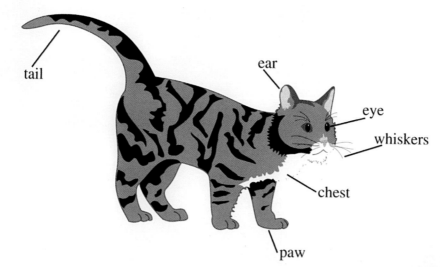

tail
ear
eye
whiskers
chest
paw

A Devon rex appears
to have very large ears.

Care

Devons have short fur and cannot stand cold or wet weather. They need to live indoors and must be kept warm. **Grooming** should be done carefully. Over brushing will cause bald spots. The best way to groom a Devon rex is with your hand or rub with a piece of silk. And Devons love every minute of it!

Like any pet, the Devon rex needs a lot of love and attention. A **scratching post** where a Devon can sharpen its claws saves furniture from damage. A cat buries its waste and should be trained to use a litter box. The box needs to be cleaned every day. Devons love to play. A ball, **catnip**, or a loose string will keep a kitten busy for hours.

Cats should be **neutered** or **spayed** unless you plan to breed them. Females can have dozens of kittens in a year. Males will spray very unpleasant odors indoors and out if not fixed.

The Devon rex is an indoor cat.

Feeding

Devons are warm to the touch. They have higher body temperatures than most cats. Because of this they need diets that are higher in fat and protein. A **veterinarian** should be able to help find the right diet for your Devon rex.

Cats are meat eaters. Hard bones that do not splinter help keep a cat's teeth and mouth clean. Water should always be available. Although they love milk, it often causes cats to become ill.

Opposite page: Devons have a higher body temperature than most cats.

Kittens

A female cat is pregnant for about 65 days. When kittens are born, there may be from three to five babies. The average Devon has four kittens. Kittens are blind and helpless for the first few weeks. Devons will be bald and look like mice.

After about three weeks, they will start crawling and playing. At this time they may be given cat food. After about a month, kittens will run, wrestle, and play games. If the cat is a **pedigree**, it should be **registered** and given papers at this time. At 10 weeks the kittens are old enough to be sold or given away.

Opposite page: Devon rex kittens are blind for the first few weeks.

Buying a Kitten

The best place to get a Devon rex is from a breeder. Cat shows are also good places to find kittens. Next you must decide if you want a simple pet or a show winner. A basic Devon can cost $100. A blue-ribbon winner can cost as much as $1,500. When you buy a Devon rex, you should get **pedigree** papers that **register** the animal with the **Cat Fanciers Association**.

When buying a kitten, check it closely for signs of good health. The ears, nose, mouth, and fur should be clean. Eyes should be bright and clear. The cat should be alert and interested in its surroundings. A healthy kitten will move around with its head held high.

A Devon rex can cost as much as $1,500.

Glossary

breed/official breed - a kind of cat; a Devon rex is a breed of cat. An official breed is a breed that is recognized by special cat organizations.

Cat Fanciers Association - a group that sets the standards for the breeds of cats.

catnip - the dried leaves and stems of a plant of the mint family, used as a stuffing for cats' toys because cats are stimulated by and drawn to its strong smell.

domestic/domesticated - tamed or adapted to home life.

Felidae - Latin name given to the cat family.

grooming - cleaning.

neutered - a male cat that is neutered cannot get a female cat pregnant.

non-pedigree - an animal without a record of its ancestors.

pedigree - a record of an animal's ancestors.

register - to add a cat to an official record of its breed.

scratching post - a post for a cat to scratch on, which is usually made out of wood or covered with carpet so the cat can wear down its nails.

spayed - a female cat that is spayed cannot have kittens.

veterinarian - an animal doctor.

Internet Sites

All About Cats
http://w3.one.net/~mich/index.html
See pictures of cats around the net, take a cat quiz to win prizes, and there is even a cat advice column. This is a fun and lively site.

Cat Fanciers Website
http://www.fanciers.com/
Information on breeds, shows, genetics, breed rescue, catteries and other topics. This is a very informative site, including clubs and many links.

Cats Homepage
http://www.cisea.it/pages/gatto/meow.htm
Page for all cat lovers. Cat photo gallery, books and more. This site has music and chat rooms, it's a lot of fun.

Cats Cats Cats
http://www.geocities.com/Heartland/Hills/5157/
This is just a fun site with pictures of cats, links, stories, and other cat stuff.

These sites are subject to change. Go to your favorite search engine and type in CATS for more sites.

PASS IT ON

Tell Others Something Special About Your Pet

To educate readers around the country, pass on interesting tips about animals, maybe a fun story about your animal or pet, and little unknown facts about animals. We want to hear from you!

To get posted on ABDO & Daughters website, E-mail us at "animals@abdopub.com"

Index